This lunch planner belongs to:

_____

 _____

Please email me if you find this notebook

BENTGO KIDS LUNCH BOX

Get your lunchbox on AMAZON
www.ashleysnotebooks.com/bentgo-kids

Copyright © 2019 by Ashley's Notebooks

All rights reserved. No part of this publication may be reproduced, distributed, or transmitted in any form or by any means, including photocopying, recording, or other electronic or mechanical methods, without the prior written permission of the publisher, except in the case of brief quotations embodied in critical reviews and certain other noncommercial uses permitted by copyright law. For permission requests, write to the publisher, addressed "Attention: Permissions Coordinator," at the address below.

info@ashleysnotebooks.com
www.ashleysnotebooks.com

school lunch
INSPIRATION

PROTEINS

- ○ turkey
- ○ ham
- ○ chicken
- ○ chickpeas
- ○ hummus
- ○ egg
- ○ yogourt
- ○ energy bites
- ○ meatballs
- ○ pepperoni
- ○ refried beans
- ○ nut butter
- ○ seed butter
- ○ Sliced lunchmeat
- ○ Blocks of cheese
- ○ Sliced cheese
- ○ Shredded cheese

FRUIT & VEG

- ○ apples
- ○ oranges
- ○ grapes
- ○ berries
- ○ watermelon
- ○ pears
- ○ apple sauce
- ○ raisins
- ○ plums
- ○ olives
- ○ cucumbers
- ○ carrots
- ○ sugar peas
- ○ carrots
- ○ celery
- ○ bell peppers
- ○ broccoli
- ○ lettuce
- ○ tomatoes

CARBS

- ○ bread
- ○ bagels
- ○ pita
- ○ tortilla
- ○ muffin
- ○ pancake
- ○ waffle
- ○ pasta
- ○ rice
- ○ crackers
- ○ pretzels
- ○ english muffin
- ○ roll
- ○ flatbread
- ○ potatoes
- ○ plantains
- ○ popcorn

SOMETHING FUN

- ○ chips
- ○ trail mix (with dark chocolate)
- ○ animal crackers
- ○ chocolate almonds
- ○ veggies straws
- ○ fruit leather
- ○ granola bar

FREE PDF DOWNLOAD
www.ashleysnotebooks.com/lunch-notes

Weekly

monday

○ Proteins ○ Carbs
○ Fruit & Veg ○ Fun

Snacks
_____
_____

Beverage
_____
_____

Rating ☆ ☆ ☆ ☆ ☆

tuesday

○ Proteins ○ Carbs
○ Fruit & Veg ○ Fun

Snacks
_____
_____

Beverage
_____
_____

Rating ☆ ☆ ☆ ☆ ☆

wednesday

○ Proteins ○ Carbs
○ Fruit & Veg ○ Fun

Snacks
_____
_____

Beverage
_____
_____

Rating ☆ ☆ ☆ ☆ ☆

lunch planner
FOR KIDS

thursday

○ Proteins ○ Carbs
○ Fruit & Veg ○ Fun

Snacks
_____
_____

Beverage
_____
_____

Rating ☆ ☆ ☆ ☆ ☆

friday

○ Proteins ○ Carbs
○ Fruit & Veg ○ Fun

Snacks
_____
_____

Beverage
_____
_____

Rating ☆ ☆ ☆ ☆ ☆

What did he/she likes?

What did he/she not like?

weekly

monday

○ Proteins ○ Carbs
○ Fruit & Veg ○ Fun

Snacks
_____
_____

Beverage
_____
_____

Rating ☆ ☆ ☆ ☆ ☆

tuesday

○ Proteins ○ Carbs
○ Fruit & Veg ○ Fun

Snacks
_____
_____

Beverage
_____
_____

Rating ☆ ☆ ☆ ☆ ☆

wednesday

○ Proteins ○ Carbs
○ Fruit & Veg ○ Fun

Snacks
_____
_____

Beverage
_____
_____

Rating ☆ ☆ ☆ ☆ ☆

lunch planner
FOR KIDS

thursday

○ Proteins ○ Carbs
○ Fruit & Veg ○ Fun

Snacks
_____
_____

Beverage
_____
_____

Rating ☆ ☆ ☆ ☆ ☆

friday

○ Proteins ○ Carbs
○ Fruit & Veg ○ Fun

Snacks
_____
_____

Beverage
_____
_____

Rating ☆ ☆ ☆ ☆ ☆

What did he/she likes?

What did he/she not like?

weekly

monday

○ Proteins ○ Carbs
○ Fruit & Veg ○ Fun

Snacks
_____
_____

Beverage
_____
_____

Rating ☆ ☆ ☆ ☆ ☆

tuesday

○ Proteins ○ Carbs
○ Fruit & Veg ○ Fun

Snacks
_____
_____

Beverage
_____
_____

Rating ☆ ☆ ☆ ☆ ☆

wednesday

○ Proteins ○ Carbs
○ Fruit & Veg ○ Fun

Snacks
_____
_____

Beverage
_____
_____

Rating ☆ ☆ ☆ ☆ ☆

lunch planner
FOR KIDS

thursday

○ Proteins ○ Carbs
○ Fruit & Veg ○ Fun

Snacks
_____
_____

Beverage
_____
_____

Rating ☆ ☆ ☆ ☆ ☆

friday

○ Proteins ○ Carbs
○ Fruit & Veg ○ Fun

Snacks
_____
_____

Beverage
_____
_____

Rating ☆ ☆ ☆ ☆ ☆

What did he/she likes?

What did he/she not like?

weekly

monday

○ Proteins   ○ Carbs
○ Fruit & Veg   ○ Fun

Snacks
_____
_____

Beverage
_____
_____

Rating ☆ ☆ ☆ ☆ ☆

tuesday

○ Proteins   ○ Carbs
○ Fruit & Veg   ○ Fun

Snacks
_____
_____

Beverage
_____
_____

Rating ☆ ☆ ☆ ☆ ☆

wednesday

○ Proteins   ○ Carbs
○ Fruit & Veg   ○ Fun

Snacks
_____
_____

Beverage
_____
_____

Rating ☆ ☆ ☆ ☆ ☆

lunch planner
FOR KIDS

thursday

○ Proteins   ○ Carbs
○ Fruit & Veg ○ Fun

Snacks
_____
_____

Beverage
_____
_____

Rating ☆ ☆ ☆ ☆ ☆

friday

○ Proteins   ○ Carbs
○ Fruit & Veg ○ Fun

Snacks
_____
_____

Beverage
_____
_____

Rating ☆ ☆ ☆ ☆ ☆

What did he/she likes?

What did he/she not like?

weekly

monday

○ Proteins   ○ Carbs
○ Fruit & Veg   ○ Fun

Snacks
_____
_____

Beverage
_____
_____

Rating ☆ ☆ ☆ ☆ ☆

tuesday

○ Proteins   ○ Carbs
○ Fruit & Veg   ○ Fun

Snacks
_____
_____

Beverage
_____
_____

Rating ☆ ☆ ☆ ☆ ☆

wednesday

○ Proteins   ○ Carbs
○ Fruit & Veg   ○ Fun

Snacks
_____
_____

Beverage
_____
_____

Rating ☆ ☆ ☆ ☆ ☆

lunch planner
FOR KIDS

thursday

○ Proteins ○ Carbs
○ Fruit & Veg ○ Fun

Snacks
_____
_____

Beverage
_____
_____

Rating ☆ ☆ ☆ ☆ ☆

friday

○ Proteins ○ Carbs
○ Fruit & Veg ○ Fun

Snacks
_____
_____

Beverage
_____
_____

Rating ☆ ☆ ☆ ☆ ☆

What did he/she likes?

What did he/she not like?

weekly

monday

○ Proteins ○ Carbs
○ Fruit & Veg ○ Fun

Snacks
_____
_____

Beverage
_____
_____

Rating ☆ ☆ ☆ ☆ ☆

tuesday

○ Proteins ○ Carbs
○ Fruit & Veg ○ Fun

Snacks
_____
_____

Beverage
_____
_____

Rating ☆ ☆ ☆ ☆ ☆

wednesday

○ Proteins ○ Carbs
○ Fruit & Veg ○ Fun

Snacks
_____
_____

Beverage
_____
_____

Rating ☆ ☆ ☆ ☆ ☆

lunch planner
FOR KIDS

thursday

○ Proteins   ○ Carbs
○ Fruit & Veg   ○ Fun

Snacks
_____
_____

Beverage
_____
_____

Rating ☆ ☆ ☆ ☆ ☆

friday

○ Proteins   ○ Carbs
○ Fruit & Veg   ○ Fun

Snacks
_____
_____

Beverage
_____
_____

Rating ☆ ☆ ☆ ☆ ☆

What did he/she likes?

What did he/she not like?

weekly

monday

- ○ Proteins ○ Carbs
- ○ Fruit & Veg ○ Fun

Snacks
_____
_____

Beverage
_____
_____

Rating ☆ ☆ ☆ ☆ ☆

tuesday

- ○ Proteins ○ Carbs
- ○ Fruit & Veg ○ Fun

Snacks
_____
_____

Beverage
_____
_____

Rating ☆ ☆ ☆ ☆ ☆

wednesday

- ○ Proteins ○ Carbs
- ○ Fruit & Veg ○ Fun

Snacks
_____
_____

Beverage
_____
_____

Rating ☆ ☆ ☆ ☆ ☆

lunch planner
FOR KIDS

thursday

○ Proteins　　○ Carbs
○ Fruit & Veg　○ Fun

Snacks
_____
_____

Beverage
_____
_____

Rating ☆ ☆ ☆ ☆ ☆

friday

○ Proteins　　○ Carbs
○ Fruit & Veg　○ Fun

Snacks
_____
_____

Beverage
_____
_____

Rating ☆ ☆ ☆ ☆ ☆

What did he/she likes?

What did he/she not like?

Weekly

monday

○ Proteins   ○ Carbs
○ Fruit & Veg   ○ Fun

Snacks
_____
_____

Beverage
_____
_____

Rating ☆ ☆ ☆ ☆ ☆

tuesday

○ Proteins   ○ Carbs
○ Fruit & Veg   ○ Fun

Snacks
_____
_____

Beverage
_____
_____

Rating ☆ ☆ ☆ ☆ ☆

wednesday

○ Proteins   ○ Carbs
○ Fruit & Veg   ○ Fun

Snacks
_____
_____

Beverage
_____
_____

Rating ☆ ☆ ☆ ☆ ☆

lunch planner
FOR KIDS

thursday

○ Proteins ○ Carbs
○ Fruit & Veg ○ Fun

Snacks
_____
_____

Beverage
_____
_____

Rating ☆ ☆ ☆ ☆ ☆

friday

○ Proteins ○ Carbs
○ Fruit & Veg ○ Fun

Snacks
_____
_____

Beverage
_____
_____

Rating ☆ ☆ ☆ ☆ ☆

What did he/she likes?

What did he/she not like?

weekly

monday

- ○ Proteins   ○ Carbs
- ○ Fruit & Veg   ○ Fun

Snacks
_____
_____

Beverage
_____
_____

Rating ☆ ☆ ☆ ☆ ☆

tuesday

- ○ Proteins   ○ Carbs
- ○ Fruit & Veg   ○ Fun

Snacks
_____
_____

Beverage
_____
_____

Rating ☆ ☆ ☆ ☆ ☆

wednesday

- ○ Proteins   ○ Carbs
- ○ Fruit & Veg   ○ Fun

Snacks
_____
_____

Beverage
_____
_____

Rating ☆ ☆ ☆ ☆ ☆

lunch planner
FOR KIDS

thursday

○ Proteins ○ Carbs
○ Fruit & Veg ○ Fun

Snacks
_____
_____

Beverage
_____
_____

Rating ☆ ☆ ☆ ☆ ☆

friday

○ Proteins ○ Carbs
○ Fruit & Veg ○ Fun

Snacks
_____
_____

Beverage
_____
_____

Rating ☆ ☆ ☆ ☆ ☆

What did he/she likes?

What did he/she not like?

weekly

monday

○ Proteins   ○ Carbs
○ Fruit & Veg ○ Fun

Snacks
_____
_____

Beverage
_____
_____

Rating ☆ ☆ ☆ ☆ ☆

tuesday

○ Proteins   ○ Carbs
○ Fruit & Veg ○ Fun

Snacks
_____
_____

Beverage
_____
_____

Rating ☆ ☆ ☆ ☆ ☆

wednesday

○ Proteins   ○ Carbs
○ Fruit & Veg ○ Fun

Snacks
_____
_____

Beverage
_____
_____

Rating ☆ ☆ ☆ ☆ ☆

lunch planner
FOR KIDS

thursday

○ Proteins   ○ Carbs
○ Fruit & Veg   ○ Fun

Snacks
_____
_____

Beverage
_____
_____

Rating ☆ ☆ ☆ ☆ ☆

friday

○ Proteins   ○ Carbs
○ Fruit & Veg   ○ Fun

Snacks
_____
_____

Beverage
_____
_____

Rating ☆ ☆ ☆ ☆ ☆

What did he/she likes?

What did he/she not like?

Weekly

monday

○ Proteins   ○ Carbs
○ Fruit & Veg   ○ Fun

Snacks
_____
_____

Beverage
_____
_____

Rating ☆ ☆ ☆ ☆ ☆

tuesday

○ Proteins   ○ Carbs
○ Fruit & Veg   ○ Fun

Snacks
_____
_____

Beverage
_____
_____

Rating ☆ ☆ ☆ ☆ ☆

wednesday

○ Proteins   ○ Carbs
○ Fruit & Veg   ○ Fun

Snacks
_____
_____

Beverage
_____
_____

Rating ☆ ☆ ☆ ☆ ☆

lunch planner
FOR KIDS

thursday

○ Proteins ○ Carbs
○ Fruit & Veg ○ Fun

Snacks
_____
_____

Beverage
_____
_____

Rating ☆ ☆ ☆ ☆ ☆

friday

○ Proteins ○ Carbs
○ Fruit & Veg ○ Fun

Snacks
_____
_____

Beverage
_____
_____

Rating ☆ ☆ ☆ ☆ ☆

What did he/she likes?

What did he/she not like?

weekly

monday

○ Proteins   ○ Carbs
○ Fruit & Veg   ○ Fun

Snacks
_____
_____

Beverage
_____
_____

Rating ☆ ☆ ☆ ☆ ☆

tuesday

○ Proteins   ○ Carbs
○ Fruit & Veg   ○ Fun

Snacks
_____
_____

Beverage
_____
_____

Rating ☆ ☆ ☆ ☆ ☆

wednesday

○ Proteins   ○ Carbs
○ Fruit & Veg   ○ Fun

Snacks
_____
_____

Beverage
_____
_____

Rating ☆ ☆ ☆ ☆ ☆

lunch planner
FOR KIDS

thursday

○ Proteins   ○ Carbs
○ Fruit & Veg   ○ Fun

Snacks
_____
_____

Beverage
_____
_____

Rating ☆ ☆ ☆ ☆ ☆

friday

○ Proteins   ○ Carbs
○ Fruit & Veg   ○ Fun

Snacks
_____
_____

Beverage
_____
_____

Rating ☆ ☆ ☆ ☆ ☆

What did he/she likes?

What did he/she not like?

weekly

monday

○ Proteins   ○ Carbs
○ Fruit & Veg   ○ Fun

Snacks
_____
_____

Beverage
_____
_____

Rating ☆ ☆ ☆ ☆ ☆

tuesday

○ Proteins   ○ Carbs
○ Fruit & Veg   ○ Fun

Snacks
_____
_____

Beverage
_____
_____

Rating ☆ ☆ ☆ ☆ ☆

wednesday

○ Proteins   ○ Carbs
○ Fruit & Veg   ○ Fun

Snacks
_____
_____

Beverage
_____
_____

Rating ☆ ☆ ☆ ☆ ☆

lunch planner
FOR KIDS

thursday

○ Proteins ○ Carbs
○ Fruit & Veg ○ Fun

Snacks
_____
_____

Beverage
_____
_____

Rating ☆ ☆ ☆ ☆ ☆

friday

○ Proteins ○ Carbs
○ Fruit & Veg ○ Fun

Snacks
_____
_____

Beverage
_____
_____

Rating ☆ ☆ ☆ ☆ ☆

What did he/she likes?

What did he/she not like?

Weekly

monday

○ Proteins ○ Carbs
○ Fruit & Veg ○ Fun

Snacks
_____
_____

Beverage
_____
_____

Rating ☆ ☆ ☆ ☆ ☆

tuesday

○ Proteins ○ Carbs
○ Fruit & Veg ○ Fun

Snacks
_____
_____

Beverage
_____
_____

Rating ☆ ☆ ☆ ☆ ☆

wednesday

○ Proteins ○ Carbs
○ Fruit & Veg ○ Fun

Snacks
_____
_____

Beverage
_____
_____

Rating ☆ ☆ ☆ ☆ ☆

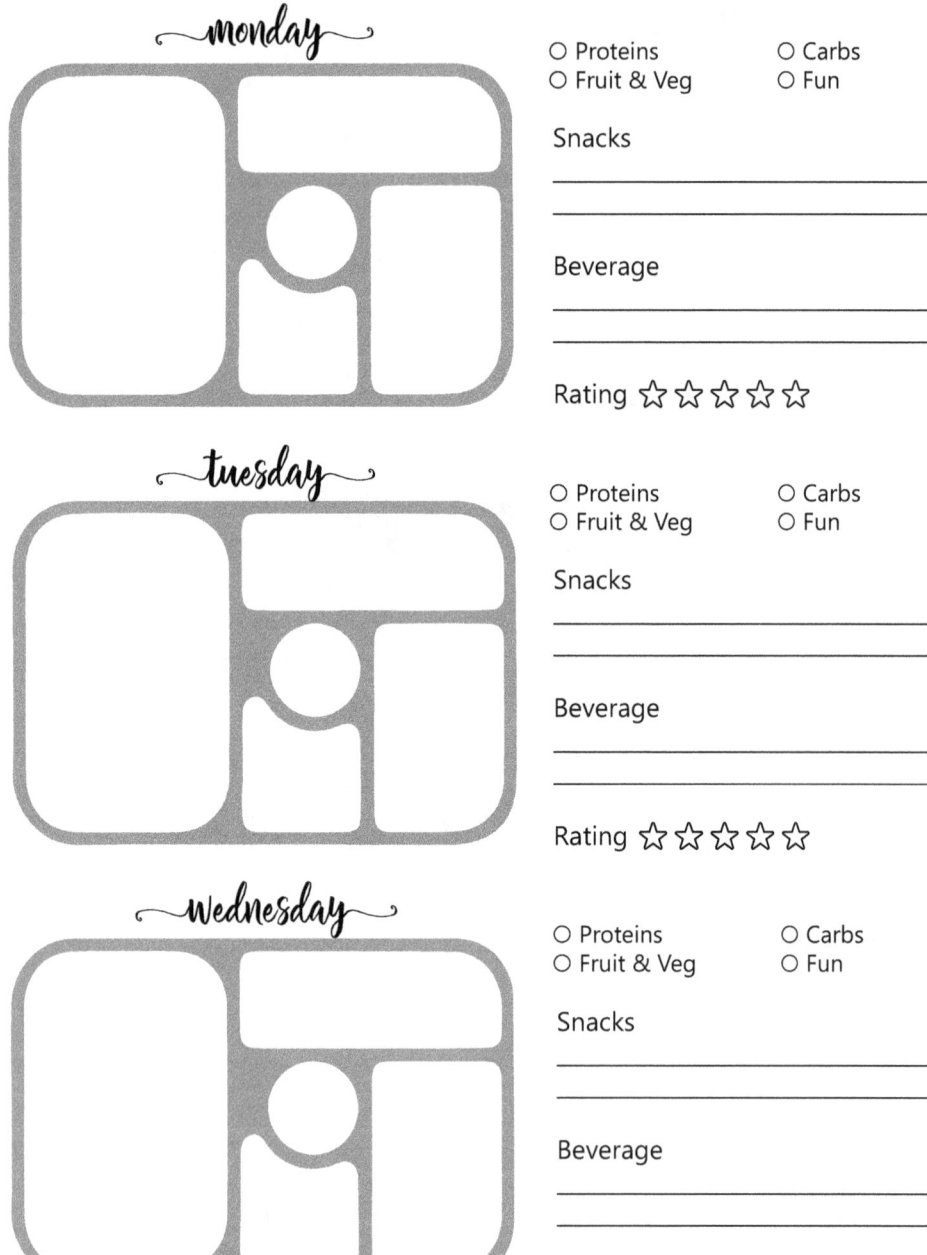

lunch planner
FOR KIDS

thursday

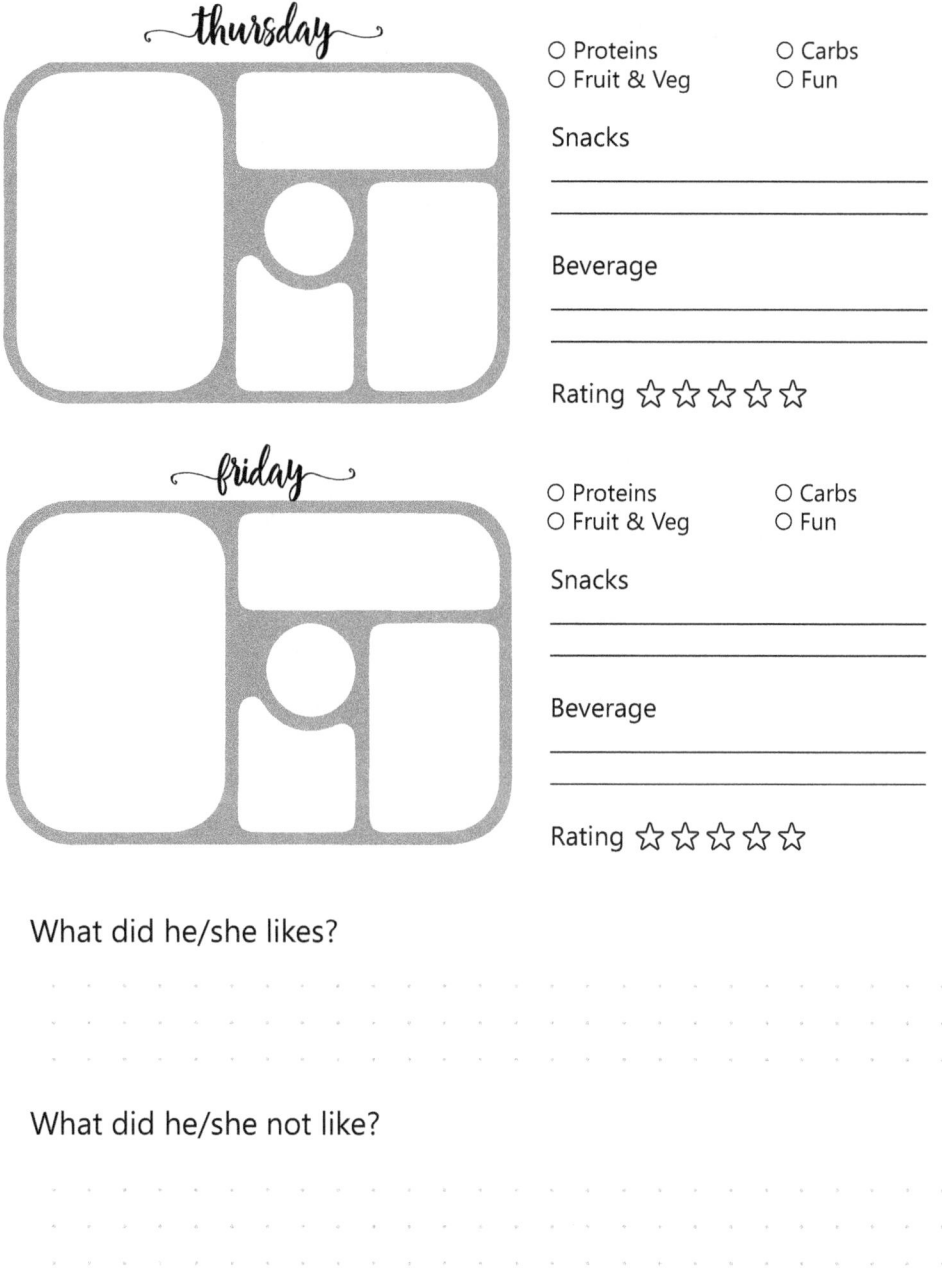

○ Proteins ○ Carbs
○ Fruit & Veg ○ Fun

Snacks
_____
_____

Beverage
_____
_____

Rating ☆ ☆ ☆ ☆ ☆

friday

○ Proteins ○ Carbs
○ Fruit & Veg ○ Fun

Snacks
_____
_____

Beverage
_____
_____

Rating ☆ ☆ ☆ ☆ ☆

What did he/she likes?

What did he/she not like?

weekly

monday

- ○ Proteins ○ Carbs
- ○ Fruit & Veg ○ Fun

Snacks
_____
_____

Beverage
_____
_____

Rating ☆☆☆☆☆

tuesday

- ○ Proteins ○ Carbs
- ○ Fruit & Veg ○ Fun

Snacks
_____
_____

Beverage
_____
_____

Rating ☆☆☆☆☆

wednesday

- ○ Proteins ○ Carbs
- ○ Fruit & Veg ○ Fun

Snacks
_____
_____

Beverage
_____
_____

Rating ☆☆☆☆☆

lunch planner
FOR KIDS

thursday

○ Proteins   ○ Carbs
○ Fruit & Veg   ○ Fun

Snacks
_____
_____

Beverage
_____
_____

Rating ☆ ☆ ☆ ☆ ☆

friday

○ Proteins   ○ Carbs
○ Fruit & Veg   ○ Fun

Snacks
_____
_____

Beverage
_____
_____

Rating ☆ ☆ ☆ ☆ ☆

What did he/she likes?

What did he/she not like?

weekly

monday

○ Proteins   ○ Carbs
○ Fruit & Veg   ○ Fun

Snacks
_____
_____

Beverage
_____
_____

Rating ☆☆☆☆☆

tuesday

○ Proteins   ○ Carbs
○ Fruit & Veg   ○ Fun

Snacks
_____
_____

Beverage
_____
_____

Rating ☆☆☆☆☆

wednesday

○ Proteins   ○ Carbs
○ Fruit & Veg   ○ Fun

Snacks
_____
_____

Beverage
_____
_____

Rating ☆☆☆☆☆

lunch planner
FOR KIDS

thursday

○ Proteins ○ Carbs
○ Fruit & Veg ○ Fun

Snacks
_____
_____

Beverage
_____
_____

Rating ☆ ☆ ☆ ☆ ☆

friday

○ Proteins ○ Carbs
○ Fruit & Veg ○ Fun

Snacks
_____
_____

Beverage
_____
_____

Rating ☆ ☆ ☆ ☆ ☆

What did he/she likes?

What did he/she not like?

Weekly

monday

○ Proteins ○ Carbs
○ Fruit & Veg ○ Fun

Snacks
_____
_____

Beverage
_____
_____

Rating ☆ ☆ ☆ ☆ ☆

tuesday

○ Proteins ○ Carbs
○ Fruit & Veg ○ Fun

Snacks
_____
_____

Beverage
_____
_____

Rating ☆ ☆ ☆ ☆ ☆

wednesday

○ Proteins ○ Carbs
○ Fruit & Veg ○ Fun

Snacks
_____
_____

Beverage
_____
_____

Rating ☆ ☆ ☆ ☆ ☆

lunch planner
FOR KIDS

thursday

○ Proteins   ○ Carbs
○ Fruit & Veg   ○ Fun

Snacks
___
___

Beverage
___
___

Rating ☆ ☆ ☆ ☆ ☆

friday

○ Proteins   ○ Carbs
○ Fruit & Veg   ○ Fun

Snacks
___
___

Beverage
___
___

Rating ☆ ☆ ☆ ☆ ☆

What did he/she likes?

What did he/she not like?

weekly

monday

○ Proteins ○ Carbs
○ Fruit & Veg ○ Fun

Snacks
_____
_____

Beverage
_____
_____

Rating ☆☆☆☆☆

tuesday

○ Proteins ○ Carbs
○ Fruit & Veg ○ Fun

Snacks
_____
_____

Beverage
_____
_____

Rating ☆☆☆☆☆

wednesday

○ Proteins ○ Carbs
○ Fruit & Veg ○ Fun

Snacks
_____
_____

Beverage
_____
_____

Rating ☆☆☆☆☆

lunch planner
FOR KIDS

thursday

○ Proteins ○ Carbs
○ Fruit & Veg ○ Fun

Snacks
_____
_____

Beverage
_____
_____

Rating ☆ ☆ ☆ ☆ ☆

friday

○ Proteins ○ Carbs
○ Fruit & Veg ○ Fun

Snacks
_____
_____

Beverage
_____
_____

Rating ☆ ☆ ☆ ☆ ☆

What did he/she likes?

What did he/she not like?

weekly

monday

- ○ Proteins ○ Carbs
- ○ Fruit & Veg ○ Fun

Snacks
_____
_____

Beverage
_____
_____

Rating ☆ ☆ ☆ ☆ ☆

tuesday

- ○ Proteins ○ Carbs
- ○ Fruit & Veg ○ Fun

Snacks
_____
_____

Beverage
_____
_____

Rating ☆ ☆ ☆ ☆ ☆

wednesday

- ○ Proteins ○ Carbs
- ○ Fruit & Veg ○ Fun

Snacks
_____
_____

Beverage
_____
_____

Rating ☆ ☆ ☆ ☆ ☆

lunch planner
FOR KIDS

thursday

○ Proteins   ○ Carbs
○ Fruit & Veg   ○ Fun

Snacks
_____
_____

Beverage
_____
_____

Rating ☆ ☆ ☆ ☆ ☆

friday

○ Proteins   ○ Carbs
○ Fruit & Veg   ○ Fun

Snacks
_____
_____

Beverage
_____
_____

Rating ☆ ☆ ☆ ☆ ☆

What did he/she likes?

What did he/she not like?

weekly

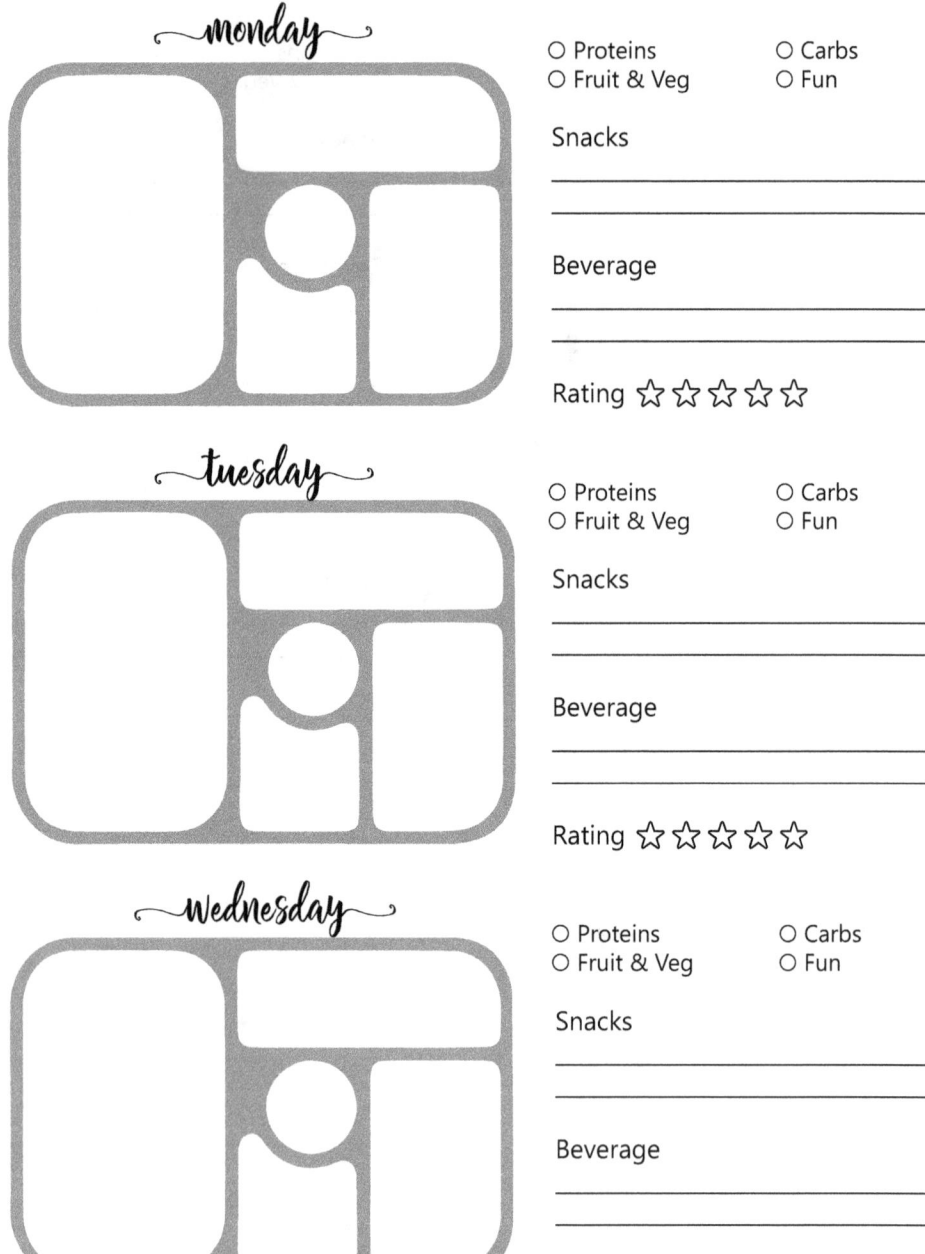

monday

○ Proteins   ○ Carbs
○ Fruit & Veg   ○ Fun

Snacks
_____
_____

Beverage
_____
_____

Rating ☆ ☆ ☆ ☆ ☆

tuesday

○ Proteins   ○ Carbs
○ Fruit & Veg   ○ Fun

Snacks
_____
_____

Beverage
_____
_____

Rating ☆ ☆ ☆ ☆ ☆

wednesday

○ Proteins   ○ Carbs
○ Fruit & Veg   ○ Fun

Snacks
_____
_____

Beverage
_____
_____

Rating ☆ ☆ ☆ ☆ ☆

lunch planner
FOR KIDS

thursday

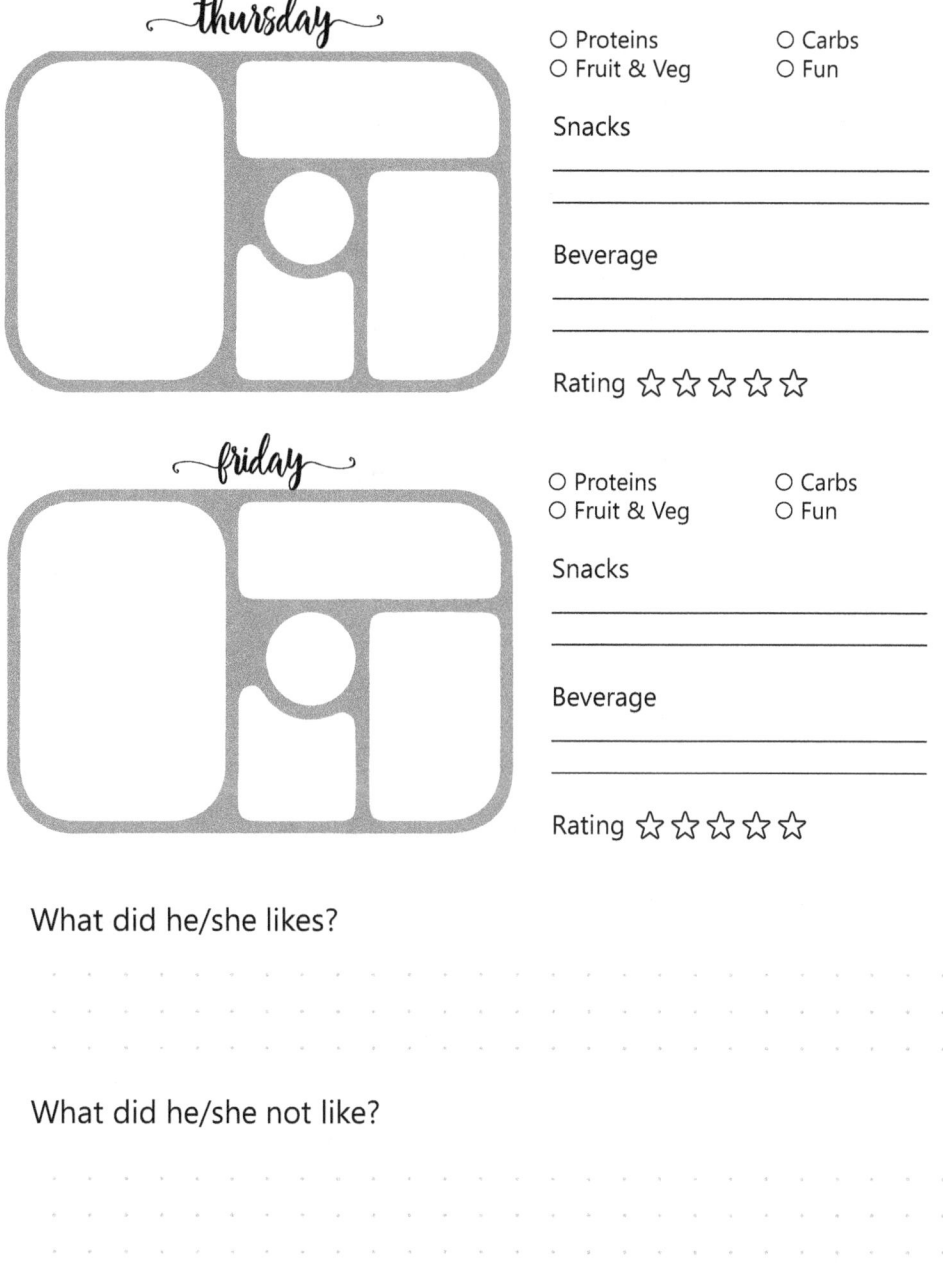

○ Proteins ○ Carbs
○ Fruit & Veg ○ Fun

Snacks
_____
_____

Beverage
_____
_____

Rating ☆ ☆ ☆ ☆ ☆

friday

○ Proteins ○ Carbs
○ Fruit & Veg ○ Fun

Snacks
_____
_____

Beverage
_____
_____

Rating ☆ ☆ ☆ ☆ ☆

What did he/she likes?

What did he/she not like?

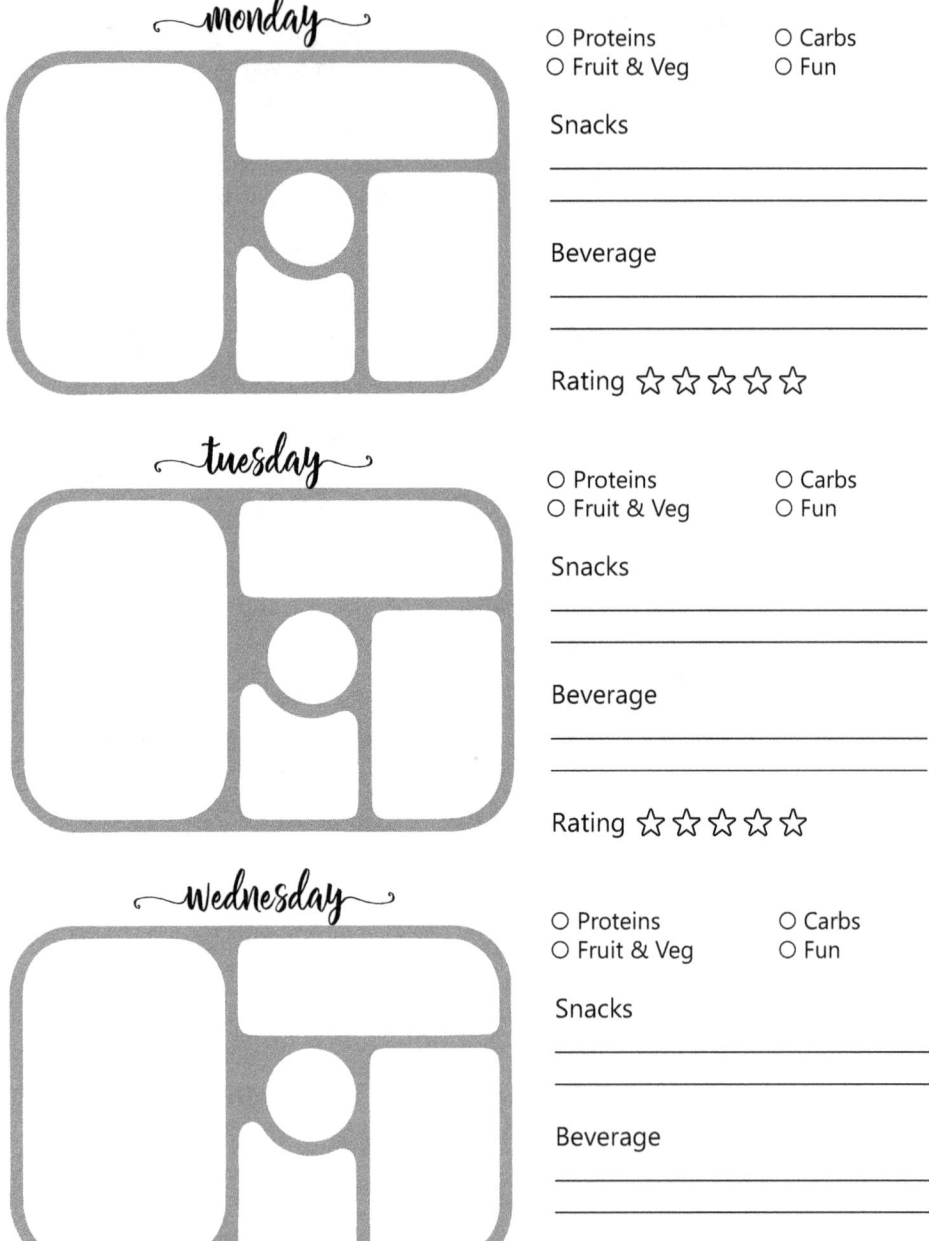

lunch planner
FOR KIDS

thursday

○ Proteins ○ Carbs
○ Fruit & Veg ○ Fun

Snacks
_____
_____

Beverage
_____
_____

Rating ☆ ☆ ☆ ☆ ☆

friday

○ Proteins ○ Carbs
○ Fruit & Veg ○ Fun

Snacks
_____
_____

Beverage
_____
_____

Rating ☆ ☆ ☆ ☆ ☆

What did he/she likes?

What did he/she not like?

weekly

monday

○ Proteins   ○ Carbs
○ Fruit & Veg   ○ Fun

Snacks
_____
_____

Beverage
_____
_____

Rating ☆ ☆ ☆ ☆ ☆

tuesday

○ Proteins   ○ Carbs
○ Fruit & Veg   ○ Fun

Snacks
_____
_____

Beverage
_____
_____

Rating ☆ ☆ ☆ ☆ ☆

wednesday

○ Proteins   ○ Carbs
○ Fruit & Veg   ○ Fun

Snacks
_____
_____

Beverage
_____
_____

Rating ☆ ☆ ☆ ☆ ☆

lunch planner
FOR KIDS

thursday

○ Proteins   ○ Carbs
○ Fruit & Veg   ○ Fun

Snacks
_____
_____

Beverage
_____
_____

Rating ☆ ☆ ☆ ☆ ☆

friday

○ Proteins   ○ Carbs
○ Fruit & Veg   ○ Fun

Snacks
_____
_____

Beverage
_____
_____

Rating ☆ ☆ ☆ ☆ ☆

What did he/she likes?

What did he/she not like?

weekly

monday

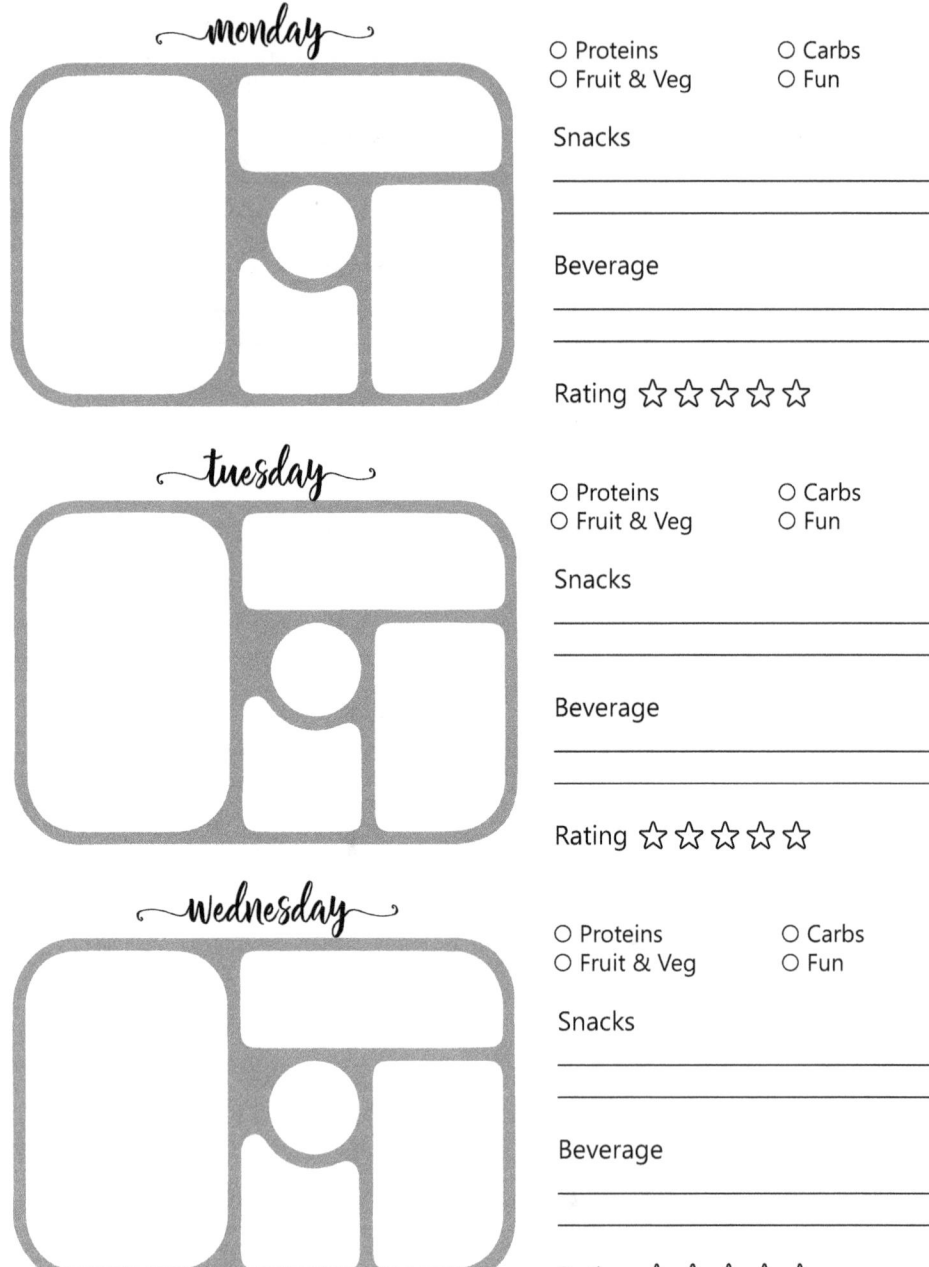

○ Proteins ○ Carbs
○ Fruit & Veg ○ Fun

Snacks
_____
_____

Beverage
_____
_____

Rating ☆ ☆ ☆ ☆ ☆

tuesday

○ Proteins ○ Carbs
○ Fruit & Veg ○ Fun

Snacks
_____
_____

Beverage
_____
_____

Rating ☆ ☆ ☆ ☆ ☆

wednesday

○ Proteins ○ Carbs
○ Fruit & Veg ○ Fun

Snacks
_____
_____

Beverage
_____
_____

Rating ☆ ☆ ☆ ☆ ☆

lunch planner
FOR KIDS

thursday

○ Proteins   ○ Carbs
○ Fruit & Veg   ○ Fun

Snacks
_____
_____

Beverage
_____
_____

Rating ☆ ☆ ☆ ☆ ☆

friday

○ Proteins   ○ Carbs
○ Fruit & Veg   ○ Fun

Snacks
_____
_____

Beverage
_____
_____

Rating ☆ ☆ ☆ ☆ ☆

What did he/she likes?

What did he/she not like?

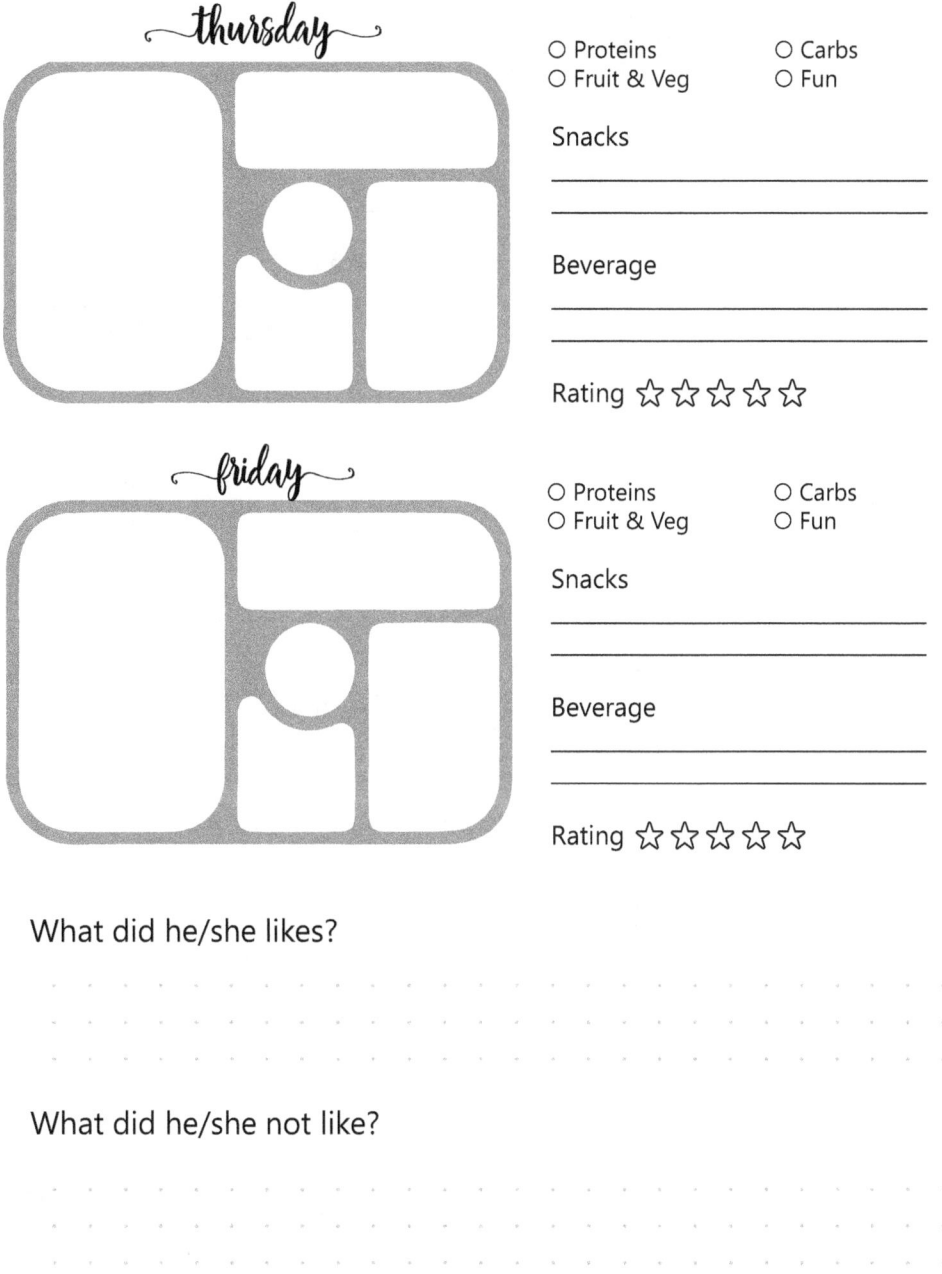

weekly

monday

○ Proteins   ○ Carbs
○ Fruit & Veg   ○ Fun

Snacks
_____
_____

Beverage
_____
_____

Rating ☆ ☆ ☆ ☆ ☆

tuesday

○ Proteins   ○ Carbs
○ Fruit & Veg   ○ Fun

Snacks
_____
_____

Beverage
_____
_____

Rating ☆ ☆ ☆ ☆ ☆

wednesday

○ Proteins   ○ Carbs
○ Fruit & Veg   ○ Fun

Snacks
_____
_____

Beverage
_____
_____

Rating ☆ ☆ ☆ ☆ ☆

lunch planner
FOR KIDS

thursday

○ Proteins   ○ Carbs
○ Fruit & Veg   ○ Fun

Snacks
_____
_____

Beverage
_____
_____

Rating ☆ ☆ ☆ ☆ ☆

friday

○ Proteins   ○ Carbs
○ Fruit & Veg   ○ Fun

Snacks
_____
_____

Beverage
_____
_____

Rating ☆ ☆ ☆ ☆ ☆

What did he/she likes?

What did he/she not like?

weekly

monday

○ Proteins ○ Carbs
○ Fruit & Veg ○ Fun

Snacks
_____
_____

Beverage
_____
_____

Rating ☆☆☆☆☆

tuesday

○ Proteins ○ Carbs
○ Fruit & Veg ○ Fun

Snacks
_____
_____

Beverage
_____
_____

Rating ☆☆☆☆☆

wednesday

○ Proteins ○ Carbs
○ Fruit & Veg ○ Fun

Snacks
_____
_____

Beverage
_____
_____

Rating ☆☆☆☆☆

lunch planner
FOR KIDS

thursday

○ Proteins ○ Carbs
○ Fruit & Veg ○ Fun

Snacks
_____
_____

Beverage
_____
_____

Rating ☆ ☆ ☆ ☆ ☆

friday

○ Proteins ○ Carbs
○ Fruit & Veg ○ Fun

Snacks
_____
_____

Beverage
_____
_____

Rating ☆ ☆ ☆ ☆ ☆

What did he/she likes?

What did he/she not like?

Weekly

monday

○ Proteins   ○ Carbs
○ Fruit & Veg   ○ Fun

Snacks
_____
_____

Beverage
_____
_____

Rating ☆☆☆☆☆

tuesday

○ Proteins   ○ Carbs
○ Fruit & Veg   ○ Fun

Snacks
_____
_____

Beverage
_____
_____

Rating ☆☆☆☆☆

wednesday

○ Proteins   ○ Carbs
○ Fruit & Veg   ○ Fun

Snacks
_____
_____

Beverage
_____
_____

Rating ☆☆☆☆☆

lunch planner
FOR KIDS

thursday

○ Proteins   ○ Carbs
○ Fruit & Veg   ○ Fun

Snacks
_____
_____

Beverage
_____
_____

Rating ☆ ☆ ☆ ☆ ☆

friday

○ Proteins   ○ Carbs
○ Fruit & Veg   ○ Fun

Snacks
_____
_____

Beverage
_____
_____

Rating ☆ ☆ ☆ ☆ ☆

What did he/she likes?

What did he/she not like?

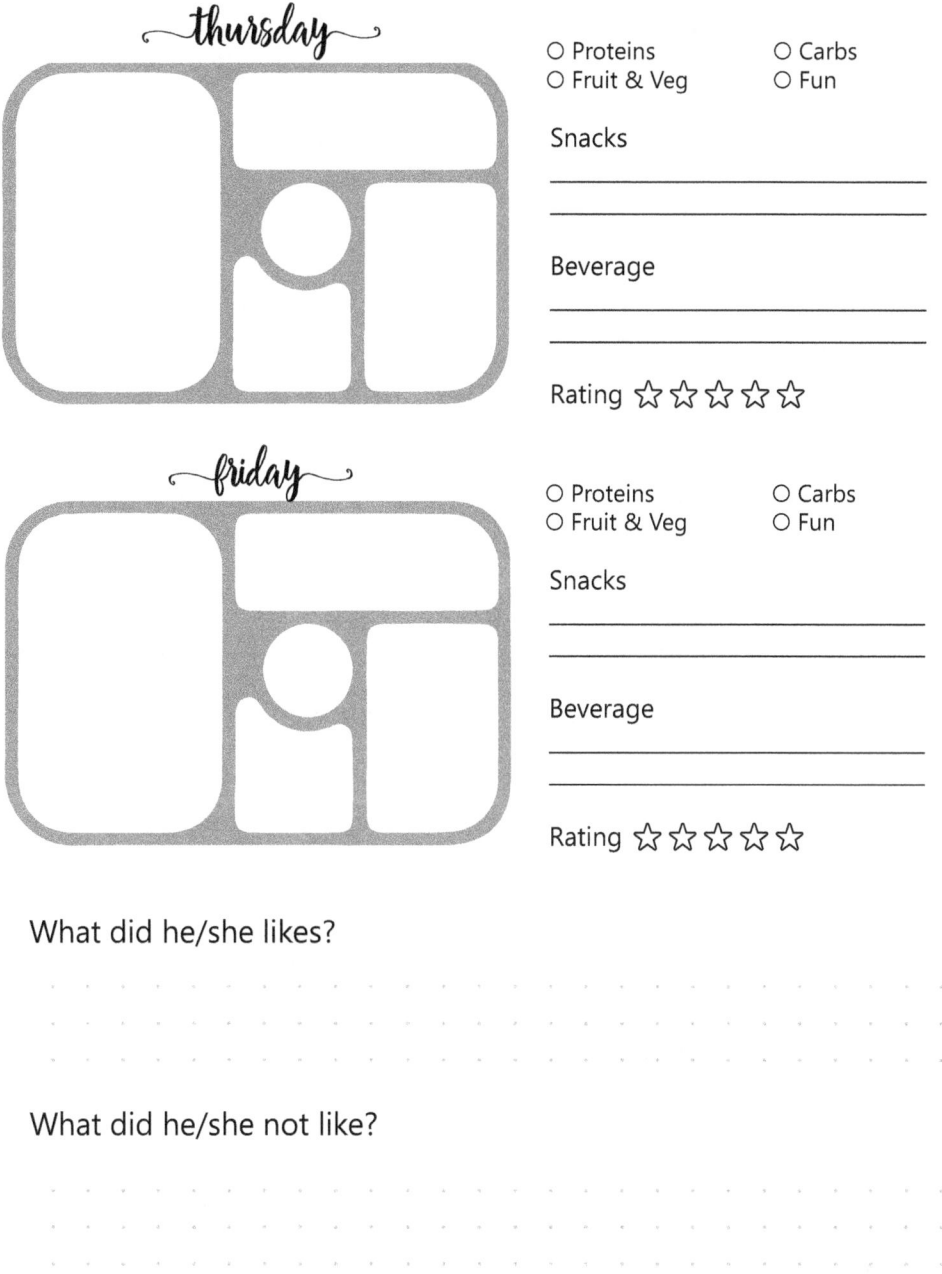

weekly

monday

○ Proteins ○ Carbs
○ Fruit & Veg ○ Fun

Snacks
_____
_____

Beverage
_____
_____

Rating ☆☆☆☆☆

tuesday

○ Proteins ○ Carbs
○ Fruit & Veg ○ Fun

Snacks
_____
_____

Beverage
_____
_____

Rating ☆☆☆☆☆

wednesday

○ Proteins ○ Carbs
○ Fruit & Veg ○ Fun

Snacks
_____
_____

Beverage
_____
_____

Rating ☆☆☆☆☆

lunch planner
FOR KIDS

thursday

○ Proteins ○ Carbs
○ Fruit & Veg ○ Fun

Snacks
_____
_____

Beverage
_____
_____

Rating ☆ ☆ ☆ ☆ ☆

friday

○ Proteins ○ Carbs
○ Fruit & Veg ○ Fun

Snacks
_____
_____

Beverage
_____
_____

Rating ☆ ☆ ☆ ☆ ☆

What did he/she likes?

What did he/she not like?

weekly

monday

○ Proteins ○ Carbs
○ Fruit & Veg ○ Fun

Snacks
_____
_____

Beverage
_____
_____

Rating ☆ ☆ ☆ ☆ ☆

tuesday

○ Proteins ○ Carbs
○ Fruit & Veg ○ Fun

Snacks
_____
_____

Beverage
_____
_____

Rating ☆ ☆ ☆ ☆ ☆

wednesday

○ Proteins ○ Carbs
○ Fruit & Veg ○ Fun

Snacks
_____
_____

Beverage
_____
_____

Rating ☆ ☆ ☆ ☆ ☆

lunch planner
FOR KIDS

thursday

○ Proteins ○ Carbs
○ Fruit & Veg ○ Fun

Snacks
_____
_____

Beverage
_____
_____

Rating ☆ ☆ ☆ ☆ ☆

friday

○ Proteins ○ Carbs
○ Fruit & Veg ○ Fun

Snacks
_____
_____

Beverage
_____
_____

Rating ☆ ☆ ☆ ☆ ☆

What did he/she likes?

What did he/she not like?

weekly

monday

○ Proteins   ○ Carbs
○ Fruit & Veg   ○ Fun

Snacks
_____
_____

Beverage
_____
_____

Rating ☆ ☆ ☆ ☆ ☆

tuesday

○ Proteins   ○ Carbs
○ Fruit & Veg   ○ Fun

Snacks
_____
_____

Beverage
_____
_____

Rating ☆ ☆ ☆ ☆ ☆

wednesday

○ Proteins   ○ Carbs
○ Fruit & Veg   ○ Fun

Snacks
_____
_____

Beverage
_____
_____

Rating ☆ ☆ ☆ ☆ ☆

lunch planner
FOR KIDS

thursday

○ Proteins   ○ Carbs
○ Fruit & Veg   ○ Fun

Snacks
_____
_____

Beverage
_____
_____

Rating ☆ ☆ ☆ ☆ ☆

friday

○ Proteins   ○ Carbs
○ Fruit & Veg   ○ Fun

Snacks
_____
_____

Beverage
_____
_____

Rating ☆ ☆ ☆ ☆ ☆

What did he/she likes?

What did he/she not like?

weekly

monday

○ Proteins ○ Carbs
○ Fruit & Veg ○ Fun

Snacks
_____
_____

Beverage
_____
_____

Rating ☆ ☆ ☆ ☆ ☆

tuesday

○ Proteins ○ Carbs
○ Fruit & Veg ○ Fun

Snacks
_____
_____

Beverage
_____
_____

Rating ☆ ☆ ☆ ☆ ☆

wednesday

○ Proteins ○ Carbs
○ Fruit & Veg ○ Fun

Snacks
_____
_____

Beverage
_____
_____

Rating ☆ ☆ ☆ ☆ ☆

lunch planner
FOR KIDS

thursday

○ Proteins ○ Carbs
○ Fruit & Veg ○ Fun

Snacks
_____
_____

Beverage
_____
_____

Rating ☆ ☆ ☆ ☆ ☆

friday

○ Proteins ○ Carbs
○ Fruit & Veg ○ Fun

Snacks
_____
_____

Beverage
_____
_____

Rating ☆ ☆ ☆ ☆ ☆

What did he/she likes?

What did he/she not like?

weekly

monday

○ Proteins   ○ Carbs
○ Fruit & Veg   ○ Fun

Snacks
_____
_____

Beverage
_____
_____

Rating ☆ ☆ ☆ ☆ ☆

tuesday

○ Proteins   ○ Carbs
○ Fruit & Veg   ○ Fun

Snacks
_____
_____

Beverage
_____
_____

Rating ☆ ☆ ☆ ☆ ☆

wednesday

○ Proteins   ○ Carbs
○ Fruit & Veg   ○ Fun

Snacks
_____
_____

Beverage
_____
_____

Rating ☆ ☆ ☆ ☆ ☆

lunch planner
FOR KIDS

thursday

○ Proteins ○ Carbs
○ Fruit & Veg ○ Fun

Snacks
_____
_____

Beverage
_____
_____

Rating ☆ ☆ ☆ ☆ ☆

friday

○ Proteins ○ Carbs
○ Fruit & Veg ○ Fun

Snacks
_____
_____

Beverage
_____
_____

Rating ☆ ☆ ☆ ☆ ☆

What did he/she likes?

What did he/she not like?

Weekly

monday

○ Proteins   ○ Carbs
○ Fruit & Veg   ○ Fun

Snacks
_____
_____

Beverage
_____
_____

Rating ☆ ☆ ☆ ☆ ☆

tuesday

○ Proteins   ○ Carbs
○ Fruit & Veg   ○ Fun

Snacks
_____
_____

Beverage
_____
_____

Rating ☆ ☆ ☆ ☆ ☆

wednesday

○ Proteins   ○ Carbs
○ Fruit & Veg   ○ Fun

Snacks
_____
_____

Beverage
_____
_____

Rating ☆ ☆ ☆ ☆ ☆

lunch planner
FOR KIDS

thursday

○ Proteins   ○ Carbs
○ Fruit & Veg   ○ Fun

Snacks
_____
_____

Beverage
_____
_____

Rating ☆☆☆☆☆

friday

○ Proteins   ○ Carbs
○ Fruit & Veg   ○ Fun

Snacks
_____
_____

Beverage
_____
_____

Rating ☆☆☆☆☆

What did he/she likes?

What did he/she not like?

weekly

monday

○ Proteins   ○ Carbs
○ Fruit & Veg   ○ Fun

Snacks
_____
_____

Beverage
_____
_____

Rating ☆☆☆☆☆

tuesday

○ Proteins   ○ Carbs
○ Fruit & Veg   ○ Fun

Snacks
_____
_____

Beverage
_____
_____

Rating ☆☆☆☆☆

wednesday

○ Proteins   ○ Carbs
○ Fruit & Veg   ○ Fun

Snacks
_____
_____

Beverage
_____
_____

Rating ☆☆☆☆☆

lunch planner
FOR KIDS

thursday

○ Proteins   ○ Carbs
○ Fruit & Veg ○ Fun

Snacks
_____
_____

Beverage
_____
_____

Rating ☆ ☆ ☆ ☆ ☆

friday

○ Proteins   ○ Carbs
○ Fruit & Veg ○ Fun

Snacks
_____
_____

Beverage
_____
_____

Rating ☆ ☆ ☆ ☆ ☆

What did he/she likes?

What did he/she not like?

weekly

monday

○ Proteins ○ Carbs
○ Fruit & Veg ○ Fun

Snacks
_____
_____

Beverage
_____
_____

Rating ☆ ☆ ☆ ☆ ☆

tuesday

○ Proteins ○ Carbs
○ Fruit & Veg ○ Fun

Snacks
_____
_____

Beverage
_____
_____

Rating ☆ ☆ ☆ ☆ ☆

wednesday

○ Proteins ○ Carbs
○ Fruit & Veg ○ Fun

Snacks
_____
_____

Beverage
_____
_____

Rating ☆ ☆ ☆ ☆ ☆

lunch planner
FOR KIDS

thursday

- ○ Proteins   ○ Carbs
- ○ Fruit & Veg   ○ Fun

Snacks
_____
_____

Beverage
_____
_____

Rating ☆ ☆ ☆ ☆ ☆

friday

- ○ Proteins   ○ Carbs
- ○ Fruit & Veg   ○ Fun

Snacks
_____
_____

Beverage
_____
_____

Rating ☆ ☆ ☆ ☆ ☆

What did he/she likes?

What did he/she not like?

Weekly

monday

○ Proteins   ○ Carbs
○ Fruit & Veg   ○ Fun

Snacks
_____
_____

Beverage
_____
_____

Rating ☆ ☆ ☆ ☆ ☆

tuesday

○ Proteins   ○ Carbs
○ Fruit & Veg   ○ Fun

Snacks
_____
_____

Beverage
_____
_____

Rating ☆ ☆ ☆ ☆ ☆

wednesday

○ Proteins   ○ Carbs
○ Fruit & Veg   ○ Fun

Snacks
_____
_____

Beverage
_____
_____

Rating ☆ ☆ ☆ ☆ ☆

lunch planner
FOR KIDS

thursday

○ Proteins ○ Carbs
○ Fruit & Veg ○ Fun

Snacks
_____
_____

Beverage
_____
_____

Rating ☆☆☆☆☆

friday

○ Proteins ○ Carbs
○ Fruit & Veg ○ Fun

Snacks
_____
_____

Beverage
_____
_____

Rating ☆☆☆☆☆

What did he/she likes?

What did he/she not like?

weekly

monday

○ Proteins   ○ Carbs
○ Fruit & Veg   ○ Fun

Snacks
_____
_____

Beverage
_____
_____

Rating ☆ ☆ ☆ ☆ ☆

tuesday

○ Proteins   ○ Carbs
○ Fruit & Veg   ○ Fun

Snacks
_____
_____

Beverage
_____
_____

Rating ☆ ☆ ☆ ☆ ☆

wednesday

○ Proteins   ○ Carbs
○ Fruit & Veg   ○ Fun

Snacks
_____
_____

Beverage
_____
_____

Rating ☆ ☆ ☆ ☆ ☆

lunch planner
FOR KIDS

thursday

○ Proteins   ○ Carbs
○ Fruit & Veg   ○ Fun

Snacks
_____
_____

Beverage
_____
_____

Rating ☆ ☆ ☆ ☆ ☆

friday

○ Proteins   ○ Carbs
○ Fruit & Veg   ○ Fun

Snacks
_____
_____

Beverage
_____
_____

Rating ☆ ☆ ☆ ☆ ☆

What did he/she likes?

What did he/she not like?

weekly

monday

○ Proteins   ○ Carbs
○ Fruit & Veg   ○ Fun

Snacks
_____
_____

Beverage
_____
_____

Rating ☆ ☆ ☆ ☆ ☆

tuesday

○ Proteins   ○ Carbs
○ Fruit & Veg   ○ Fun

Snacks
_____
_____

Beverage
_____
_____

Rating ☆ ☆ ☆ ☆ ☆

wednesday

○ Proteins   ○ Carbs
○ Fruit & Veg   ○ Fun

Snacks
_____
_____

Beverage
_____
_____

Rating ☆ ☆ ☆ ☆ ☆

lunch planner
FOR KIDS

thursday

○ Proteins   ○ Carbs
○ Fruit & Veg   ○ Fun

Snacks
_____
_____

Beverage
_____
_____

Rating ☆ ☆ ☆ ☆ ☆

friday

○ Proteins   ○ Carbs
○ Fruit & Veg   ○ Fun

Snacks
_____
_____

Beverage
_____
_____

Rating ☆ ☆ ☆ ☆ ☆

What did he/she likes?

What did he/she not like?

weekly

monday

- ○ Proteins   ○ Carbs
- ○ Fruit & Veg ○ Fun

Snacks
_____
_____

Beverage
_____
_____

Rating ☆ ☆ ☆ ☆ ☆

tuesday

- ○ Proteins   ○ Carbs
- ○ Fruit & Veg ○ Fun

Snacks
_____
_____

Beverage
_____
_____

Rating ☆ ☆ ☆ ☆ ☆

wednesday

- ○ Proteins   ○ Carbs
- ○ Fruit & Veg ○ Fun

Snacks
_____
_____

Beverage
_____
_____

Rating ☆ ☆ ☆ ☆ ☆

lunch planner
FOR KIDS

thursday

○ Proteins   ○ Carbs
○ Fruit & Veg   ○ Fun

Snacks
_____
_____

Beverage
_____
_____

Rating ☆ ☆ ☆ ☆ ☆

friday

○ Proteins   ○ Carbs
○ Fruit & Veg   ○ Fun

Snacks
_____
_____

Beverage
_____
_____

Rating ☆ ☆ ☆ ☆ ☆

What did he/she likes?

What did he/she not like?

weekly

monday

○ Proteins ○ Carbs
○ Fruit & Veg ○ Fun

Snacks
_____
_____

Beverage
_____
_____

Rating ☆☆☆☆☆

tuesday

○ Proteins ○ Carbs
○ Fruit & Veg ○ Fun

Snacks
_____
_____

Beverage
_____
_____

Rating ☆☆☆☆☆

wednesday

○ Proteins ○ Carbs
○ Fruit & Veg ○ Fun

Snacks
_____
_____

Beverage
_____
_____

Rating ☆☆☆☆☆

lunch planner
FOR KIDS

thursday

- ○ Proteins ○ Carbs
- ○ Fruit & Veg ○ Fun

Snacks
_____
_____

Beverage
_____
_____

Rating ☆ ☆ ☆ ☆ ☆

friday

- ○ Proteins ○ Carbs
- ○ Fruit & Veg ○ Fun

Snacks
_____
_____

Beverage
_____
_____

Rating ☆ ☆ ☆ ☆ ☆

What did he/she likes?

What did he/she not like?

weekly

monday

○ Proteins   ○ Carbs
○ Fruit & Veg ○ Fun

Snacks
_____
_____

Beverage
_____
_____

Rating ☆ ☆ ☆ ☆ ☆

tuesday

○ Proteins   ○ Carbs
○ Fruit & Veg ○ Fun

Snacks
_____
_____

Beverage
_____
_____

Rating ☆ ☆ ☆ ☆ ☆

wednesday

○ Proteins   ○ Carbs
○ Fruit & Veg ○ Fun

Snacks
_____
_____

Beverage
_____
_____

Rating ☆ ☆ ☆ ☆ ☆

lunch planner
FOR KIDS

thursday

○ Proteins   ○ Carbs
○ Fruit & Veg   ○ Fun

Snacks
_____
_____

Beverage
_____
_____

Rating ☆ ☆ ☆ ☆ ☆

friday

○ Proteins   ○ Carbs
○ Fruit & Veg   ○ Fun

Snacks
_____
_____

Beverage
_____
_____

Rating ☆ ☆ ☆ ☆ ☆

What did he/she likes?

What did he/she not like?

weekly

monday

○ Proteins ○ Carbs
○ Fruit & Veg ○ Fun

Snacks
_____
_____

Beverage
_____
_____

Rating ☆ ☆ ☆ ☆ ☆

tuesday

○ Proteins ○ Carbs
○ Fruit & Veg ○ Fun

Snacks
_____
_____

Beverage
_____
_____

Rating ☆ ☆ ☆ ☆ ☆

wednesday

○ Proteins ○ Carbs
○ Fruit & Veg ○ Fun

Snacks
_____
_____

Beverage
_____
_____

Rating ☆ ☆ ☆ ☆ ☆

lunch planner
FOR KIDS

thursday

○ Proteins ○ Carbs
○ Fruit & Veg ○ Fun

Snacks
_____
_____

Beverage
_____
_____

Rating ☆ ☆ ☆ ☆ ☆

friday

○ Proteins ○ Carbs
○ Fruit & Veg ○ Fun

Snacks
_____
_____

Beverage
_____
_____

Rating ☆ ☆ ☆ ☆ ☆

What did he/she likes?

What did he/she not like?

weekly

monday

- ○ Proteins   ○ Carbs
- ○ Fruit & Veg   ○ Fun

Snacks
_____
_____

Beverage
_____
_____

Rating ☆ ☆ ☆ ☆ ☆

tuesday

- ○ Proteins   ○ Carbs
- ○ Fruit & Veg   ○ Fun

Snacks
_____
_____

Beverage
_____
_____

Rating ☆ ☆ ☆ ☆ ☆

wednesday

- ○ Proteins   ○ Carbs
- ○ Fruit & Veg   ○ Fun

Snacks
_____
_____

Beverage
_____
_____

Rating ☆ ☆ ☆ ☆ ☆

lunch planner
FOR KIDS

thursday

○ Proteins   ○ Carbs
○ Fruit & Veg   ○ Fun

Snacks
_____
_____

Beverage
_____
_____

Rating ☆ ☆ ☆ ☆ ☆

friday

○ Proteins   ○ Carbs
○ Fruit & Veg   ○ Fun

Snacks
_____
_____

Beverage
_____
_____

Rating ☆ ☆ ☆ ☆ ☆

What did he/she likes?

What did he/she not like?

weekly

monday

- ○ Proteins
- ○ Fruit & Veg
- ○ Carbs
- ○ Fun

Snacks
_____
_____

Beverage
_____
_____

Rating ☆ ☆ ☆ ☆ ☆

tuesday

- ○ Proteins
- ○ Fruit & Veg
- ○ Carbs
- ○ Fun

Snacks
_____
_____

Beverage
_____
_____

Rating ☆ ☆ ☆ ☆ ☆

wednesday

- ○ Proteins
- ○ Fruit & Veg
- ○ Carbs
- ○ Fun

Snacks
_____
_____

Beverage
_____
_____

Rating ☆ ☆ ☆ ☆ ☆

lunch planner
FOR KIDS

thursday

○ Proteins   ○ Carbs
○ Fruit & Veg   ○ Fun

Snacks
_____
_____

Beverage
_____
_____

Rating ☆ ☆ ☆ ☆ ☆

friday

○ Proteins   ○ Carbs
○ Fruit & Veg   ○ Fun

Snacks
_____
_____

Beverage
_____
_____

Rating ☆ ☆ ☆ ☆ ☆

What did he/she likes?

What did he/she not like?

Weekly

monday

○ Proteins   ○ Carbs
○ Fruit & Veg   ○ Fun

Snacks
_____
_____

Beverage
_____
_____

Rating ☆ ☆ ☆ ☆ ☆

tuesday

○ Proteins   ○ Carbs
○ Fruit & Veg   ○ Fun

Snacks
_____
_____

Beverage
_____
_____

Rating ☆ ☆ ☆ ☆ ☆

wednesday

○ Proteins   ○ Carbs
○ Fruit & Veg   ○ Fun

Snacks
_____
_____

Beverage
_____
_____

Rating ☆ ☆ ☆ ☆ ☆

lunch planner
FOR KIDS

thursday

○ Proteins ○ Carbs
○ Fruit & Veg ○ Fun

Snacks
_____
_____

Beverage
_____
_____

Rating ☆☆☆☆☆

friday

○ Proteins ○ Carbs
○ Fruit & Veg ○ Fun

Snacks
_____
_____

Beverage
_____
_____

Rating ☆☆☆☆☆

What did he/she likes?

What did he/she not like?

weekly

monday

○ Proteins ○ Carbs
○ Fruit & Veg ○ Fun

Snacks
_____
_____

Beverage
_____
_____

Rating ☆☆☆☆☆

tuesday

○ Proteins ○ Carbs
○ Fruit & Veg ○ Fun

Snacks
_____
_____

Beverage
_____
_____

Rating ☆☆☆☆☆

wednesday

○ Proteins ○ Carbs
○ Fruit & Veg ○ Fun

Snacks
_____
_____

Beverage
_____
_____

Rating ☆☆☆☆☆

lunch planner
FOR KIDS

thursday

○ Proteins ○ Carbs
○ Fruit & Veg ○ Fun

Snacks
_____
_____

Beverage
_____
_____

Rating ☆ ☆ ☆ ☆ ☆

friday

○ Proteins ○ Carbs
○ Fruit & Veg ○ Fun

Snacks
_____
_____

Beverage
_____
_____

Rating ☆ ☆ ☆ ☆ ☆

What did he/she likes?

What did he/she not like?

weekly

monday

○ Proteins   ○ Carbs
○ Fruit & Veg ○ Fun

Snacks
_____
_____

Beverage
_____
_____

Rating ☆ ☆ ☆ ☆ ☆

tuesday

○ Proteins   ○ Carbs
○ Fruit & Veg ○ Fun

Snacks
_____
_____

Beverage
_____
_____

Rating ☆ ☆ ☆ ☆ ☆

wednesday

○ Proteins   ○ Carbs
○ Fruit & Veg ○ Fun

Snacks
_____
_____

Beverage
_____
_____

Rating ☆ ☆ ☆ ☆ ☆

lunch planner
FOR KIDS

thursday

○ Proteins　　○ Carbs
○ Fruit & Veg　○ Fun

Snacks
_____
_____

Beverage
_____
_____

Rating ☆ ☆ ☆ ☆ ☆

friday

○ Proteins　　○ Carbs
○ Fruit & Veg　○ Fun

Snacks
_____
_____

Beverage
_____
_____

Rating ☆ ☆ ☆ ☆ ☆

What did he/she likes?

What did he/she not like?

weekly

monday

○ Proteins ○ Carbs
○ Fruit & Veg ○ Fun

Snacks
_____
_____

Beverage
_____
_____

Rating ☆ ☆ ☆ ☆ ☆

tuesday

○ Proteins ○ Carbs
○ Fruit & Veg ○ Fun

Snacks
_____
_____

Beverage
_____
_____

Rating ☆ ☆ ☆ ☆ ☆

wednesday

○ Proteins ○ Carbs
○ Fruit & Veg ○ Fun

Snacks
_____
_____

Beverage
_____
_____

Rating ☆ ☆ ☆ ☆ ☆

lunch planner
FOR KIDS

thursday

○ Proteins ○ Carbs
○ Fruit & Veg ○ Fun

Snacks
_____
_____

Beverage
_____
_____

Rating ☆ ☆ ☆ ☆ ☆

friday

○ Proteins ○ Carbs
○ Fruit & Veg ○ Fun

Snacks
_____
_____

Beverage
_____
_____

Rating ☆ ☆ ☆ ☆ ☆

What did he/she likes?

What did he/she not like?

weekly

monday

○ Proteins ○ Carbs
○ Fruit & Veg ○ Fun

Snacks
_____
_____

Beverage
_____
_____

Rating ☆☆☆☆☆

tuesday

○ Proteins ○ Carbs
○ Fruit & Veg ○ Fun

Snacks
_____
_____

Beverage
_____
_____

Rating ☆☆☆☆☆

wednesday

○ Proteins ○ Carbs
○ Fruit & Veg ○ Fun

Snacks
_____
_____

Beverage
_____
_____

Rating ☆☆☆☆☆

lunch planner
FOR KIDS

thursday

○ Proteins　　○ Carbs
○ Fruit & Veg　○ Fun

Snacks
_____
_____

Beverage
_____
_____

Rating ☆ ☆ ☆ ☆ ☆

friday

○ Proteins　　○ Carbs
○ Fruit & Veg　○ Fun

Snacks
_____
_____

Beverage
_____
_____

Rating ☆ ☆ ☆ ☆ ☆

What did he/she likes?

What did he/she not like?

weekly

monday

○ Proteins ○ Carbs
○ Fruit & Veg ○ Fun

Snacks
_____
_____

Beverage
_____
_____

Rating ☆ ☆ ☆ ☆ ☆

tuesday

○ Proteins ○ Carbs
○ Fruit & Veg ○ Fun

Snacks
_____
_____

Beverage
_____
_____

Rating ☆ ☆ ☆ ☆ ☆

wednesday

○ Proteins ○ Carbs
○ Fruit & Veg ○ Fun

Snacks
_____
_____

Beverage
_____
_____

Rating ☆ ☆ ☆ ☆ ☆

lunch planner
FOR KIDS

thursday

○ Proteins   ○ Carbs
○ Fruit & Veg ○ Fun

Snacks
_____
_____

Beverage
_____
_____

Rating ☆ ☆ ☆ ☆ ☆

friday

○ Proteins   ○ Carbs
○ Fruit & Veg ○ Fun

Snacks
_____
_____

Beverage
_____
_____

Rating ☆ ☆ ☆ ☆ ☆

What did he/she likes?

What did he/she not like?

weekly

monday

○ Proteins ○ Carbs
○ Fruit & Veg ○ Fun

Snacks
_____
_____

Beverage
_____
_____

Rating ☆ ☆ ☆ ☆ ☆

tuesday

○ Proteins ○ Carbs
○ Fruit & Veg ○ Fun

Snacks
_____
_____

Beverage
_____
_____

Rating ☆ ☆ ☆ ☆ ☆

wednesday

○ Proteins ○ Carbs
○ Fruit & Veg ○ Fun

Snacks
_____
_____

Beverage
_____
_____

Rating ☆ ☆ ☆ ☆ ☆

lunch planner
FOR KIDS

thursday

○ Proteins ○ Carbs
○ Fruit & Veg ○ Fun

Snacks
_____
_____

Beverage
_____
_____

Rating ☆ ☆ ☆ ☆ ☆

friday

○ Proteins ○ Carbs
○ Fruit & Veg ○ Fun

Snacks
_____
_____

Beverage
_____
_____

Rating ☆ ☆ ☆ ☆ ☆

What did he/she likes?

What did he/she not like?

weekly

monday

- ○ Proteins
- ○ Fruit & Veg
- ○ Carbs
- ○ Fun

Snacks
_____
_____

Beverage
_____
_____

Rating ☆☆☆☆☆

tuesday

- ○ Proteins
- ○ Fruit & Veg
- ○ Carbs
- ○ Fun

Snacks
_____
_____

Beverage
_____
_____

Rating ☆☆☆☆☆

wednesday

- ○ Proteins
- ○ Fruit & Veg
- ○ Carbs
- ○ Fun

Snacks
_____
_____

Beverage
_____
_____

Rating ☆☆☆☆☆

lunch planner
FOR KIDS

thursday

○ Proteins   ○ Carbs
○ Fruit & Veg ○ Fun

Snacks
_____
_____

Beverage
_____
_____

Rating ☆ ☆ ☆ ☆ ☆

friday

○ Proteins   ○ Carbs
○ Fruit & Veg ○ Fun

Snacks
_____
_____

Beverage
_____
_____

Rating ☆ ☆ ☆ ☆ ☆

What did he/she likes?

What did he/she not like?

weekly

monday

- ○ Proteins ○ Carbs
- ○ Fruit & Veg ○ Fun

Snacks
_____
_____

Beverage
_____
_____

Rating ☆ ☆ ☆ ☆ ☆

tuesday

- ○ Proteins ○ Carbs
- ○ Fruit & Veg ○ Fun

Snacks
_____
_____

Beverage
_____
_____

Rating ☆ ☆ ☆ ☆ ☆

wednesday

- ○ Proteins ○ Carbs
- ○ Fruit & Veg ○ Fun

Snacks
_____
_____

Beverage
_____
_____

Rating ☆ ☆ ☆ ☆ ☆

lunch planner
FOR KIDS

thursday

○ Proteins   ○ Carbs
○ Fruit & Veg   ○ Fun

Snacks
_____
_____

Beverage
_____
_____

Rating ☆ ☆ ☆ ☆ ☆

friday

○ Proteins   ○ Carbs
○ Fruit & Veg   ○ Fun

Snacks
_____
_____

Beverage
_____
_____

Rating ☆ ☆ ☆ ☆ ☆

What did he/she likes?

What did he/she not like?

notes

notes

exclusive bonus

Download our interactive PDF grocery list.
Fill the pdf on your computer and print a clean list
or
print blank pages

Use this link : **www.ashleysnotebooks.com/grocery**

CPSIA information can be obtained
at www.ICGtesting.com
Printed in the USA
LVHW081251270819
629098LV00015B/297/P